MARVIN TERBAN

PUNCHING THE CLOCK

Funny Action Idioms

illustrated by
TOM HUFFMAN

CLARION BOOKS

NEW YORK

To my dear cousin Sybil C. Simon
and
my funny uncle Henny Youngman,
two action idioms who never stop punching the clock
—M.T.

Joy to Michael Nathan and A.J.
—T.H.

Clarion Books
a Houghton Mifflin Company imprint
215 Park Avenue South, New York, N.Y. 10003
Text copyright © 1990 by Marvin Terban
Illustrations copyright © 1990 by Tom Huffman
All rights reserved. For information about permission to
reproduce selections from this book, write to Permissions,
Houghton Mifflin Company, 2 Park Street, Boston, MA 02108.
Printed in the USA
Library of Congress Cataloging-in-Publication Data
Terban, Marvin.
Punching the clock : funny action idioms / by Marvin Terban :
illustrated by Tom Huffman.
p. cm.
Includes bibliographical references.
Summary: Introduces and explains almost 100 expressions which
mean something different than the separate words in the group. For
example: raise the roof, hold your horses, and beat the bushes.
ISBN 0-89919-864-3—ISBN 0-89919-865-1 (pbk.)
1. English language—Idioms—Juvenile literature. [1.English
language—Idioms.] I. Huffman, Tom, ill. II. Title.
PE 1460. T388 1990
428.1—dc20
89-38087
CIP
AC

HC BP PA ALP 10 9 8 7 6 5 4 3 2 1

Contents

Introduction

Idioms are fun and useful phrases, but they can also be confusing. An idiom is a group of words, but the words don't mean together what they mean by themselves. That's what makes idioms so confusing.

For instance, someone says that something's "driving him up the wall," and he's going to "raise the roof." He really means that something is making him furious, and he's going to make a loud disturbance. As you can see, the meaning of an idiom can have little or nothing to do with the separate meanings of the words in the idiom.

As a language develops over hundreds of years, people make up idioms to suit special needs. They often use dynamic words that relate to sports, physical exercise, or action (such as *lift, push, pull, throw, hit, catch, run, jump,* and *kick)* to express everyday ideas. These words convey powerful, energetic images, and they keep our language lively.

This book will introduce and explain almost one hundred of these vivid expressions. Word experts don't always agree on where these idioms came from, but we've included some of the most interesting origins.

Now, when you hear or read one of these action idioms, you won't have to "jump to conclusions," "raise Cain," or be "bowled over." You'll "bat a thousand"!

So let's not "beat around the bush." Let's "pull out all the stops." You may not know all these idioms now, but after reading this book, they'll all "strike a familiar chord." Are you "catching on"?

° 1 °

Lift, Raise, Carry

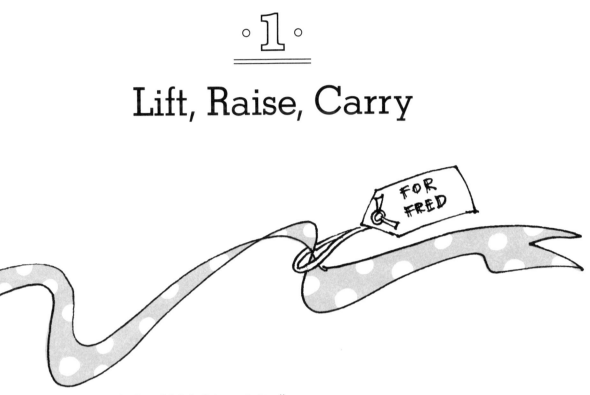

1. "This gift should **lift his spirits**."
   This gift should make him feel better.

   ■ When someone feels bad about something, we say he's "downhearted" or "down in the dumps" or "down and out" or that "his spirits are down." When someone feels great, we say he's "upbeat" or he's "feeling up" or his "spirits are up." How do you get something that's down back up? You give it a lift. Then you feel "uplifted."

2. "We do all the work, and she won't even **lift a finger to help**!"
   She won't help at all.

   ■ How much help can you give with just one finger? Not much, right? Well, a person who won't even lift one little finger to help you isn't even making the tiniest effort to do his or her share.

3. "When he sees this bill, he'll definitely **raise Cain**."
   He'll be tremendously angry and cause a lot of trouble.

   ■ In the Bible, Cain, one of the sons of Adam and Eve, got so bitterly jealous of his brother, Abel, that he killed him. Today, we say someone who is behaving violently, protesting angrily, or disturbing noisily is "raising Cain." By the way, "raising havoc" is the same as "raising Cain."

4. "Well, that will really **raise some eyebrows**."
   That will surprise or shock some people.

   ■ Did you ever see someone who was really surprised? Did his chin drop down? Did his eyebrows fly up? Surprise someone today. See what happens. Raise somebody's eyebrows. But don't do anything too shocking.

5. "When he broke her favorite toy, she started to **raise the roof**."
She expressed her anger loudly.

■ Imagine a person exploding with noisy complaints. What would this uproar do to the roof? It would lift it right off its rafters, wouldn't it? Add "raise the roof" to "raise Cain" and "raise havoc" as another lively idiom for expressing anger.

6. "It's obvious that she's **carrying the torch** for him."
She's suffering because she loves him and he doesn't love her back.

■ Venus, the goddess of love, carried a torch. That torch became the symbol of loyalty, then love, then burning devotion. So it's easy to see that if you "carry a torch" for someone it means that you love him or her. But if that person doesn't carry a torch for you, you'll be awfully sad.

7. "You have to **carry the ball** in this project."
We depend on you to do most of the work.

■ This idiom probably comes from football, where the player who carries the ball is doing a lot of the work, usually the most important or most difficult part of the play.

8. "He looks as though he's **carrying the weight of the world on his shoulders**."
He looks extremely worried.

■ In an ancient Greek myth, a giant named Atlas revolted against the ruler of the gods, Zeus. Zeus punished him by making him carry all the heavens on his shoulders. Maybe you've seen a statue or a picture of poor Atlas struggling under his tremendous burden. Well, today when an ordinary person has a heavy load of responsibility and looks very tired or worried, we say that he's "carrying the world on his shoulders" just as Atlas did.

9. "How did he get into the chorus? He can't **carry a tune**."
He can't sing on pitch.

■ Of course, you sing, hum, or whistle a tune, not carry it. But pitch (the highness or lowness of a sound) is something you have to keep up or keep down. You can't drop it. You've got to hold onto it. You've got to "carry" it. Otherwise, when you open your mouth, people will cover their ears!

10. "She **carried on** terribly when he **carried on carrying on**."
She was very sad when he continued misbehaving.

■ Here's a triple-play idiom. It has three different common meanings. First, it can mean to weep, grieve, or be hysterically sad. ("She carried on for hours when she heard the bad news.") It can also mean to keep on doing something. ("Carry on with your work.") Finally, it can mean to behave badly. ("He carried on like a wild animal and almost got arrested.") One idiom with three meanings. That's a lot of carrying on!

Push, Pull, Play

11. "If the lion gets out, don't **push the panic button**."
Don't become terrified.

■ A button marked "panic" doesn't really exist, but pretend it does. Now pretend something dangerous or nerve-wracking happens. Instead of taking care of the problem calmly, you become frightened, lose your head, and "push the panic button." Now there's a general emergency. Everyone is nervous, worried, and overexcited. You have to "pull yourself together."

12. "The emergency is over. Now **pull yourself together**."
Recover your self-control.

■ OK. You got scared and "pushed the panic button." You lost your head and maybe your mind. Now get a grip on yourself. Go find your lost head and the other parts and "pull yourself together."

13. "Everything was OK until they **pulled the rug out from under him**."
They unexpectedly spoiled his plans.

■ When someone stands on a solid floor, he usually feels secure. But if he's really standing on a slippery rug, and someone yanks that rug out from under him, what happens? He comes crashing down. Well, think of someone who feels that things are going his way. Then suddenly someone withdraws support or sabotages his plans. He's had "the rug pulled out from under him." Kerplunk!

14. "They **pulled a fast one** on her."
    They fooled her.

    ■ This idiom might have come from the art of magic. Often, a magician will pull something out of a pocket, a box, or a hat so quickly that the audience doesn't see it. The audience has been tricked. Today, we use the same idea to express the act of fooling or cheating someone. The sneaky trickster does it so fast that the person being tricked doesn't even realize what's happening.

15. "We've got to get this job done. Let's **pull out all the stops**!"
    Let's do everything we can. Hold nothing back.

    ■ Did you ever see a big pipe organ? It probably had lots of knobs (called "stops"). The organist pushed some stops in to block the sound of some pipes. When he wanted to play a huge sound, he pulled out all the stops. Now, if you use everything you've got—all your resources, time, energy, talents, and strength—to get some huge task accomplished, you, too, are "pulling out all the stops."

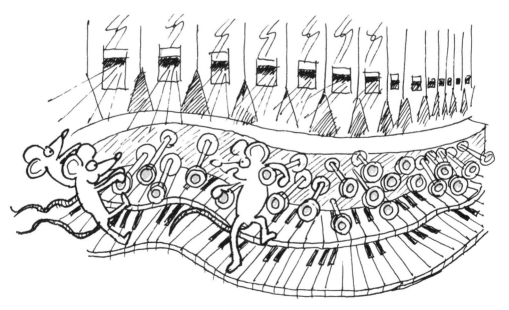

16. "The teacher is furious, and she will **pull no punches**."
She won't be nice and hold anything back.

■ You've probably figured out that this idiom came from boxing. When a boxer lets a walloping punch fly, watch out! But if he doesn't hit as hard as he could, then he's pulling back on his punches. If you speak or act in a gentle way when you could have acted harshly, you are "pulling your punches." But if you act strictly and severely, you're pulling no punches. Watch out!

17. "To get these front row seats, I had to **pull some strings**."
I had to use my personal influence with some people.

■ Think of a puppeteer. He pulls the strings that make the puppets move. But the audience can't see the "string puller" behind the scenes. If someone secretly exerts power to get people to do what he wants, then he's "pulling strings" like the puppeteer.

18. "After living here for many years, he's finally **pulling up stakes**."
He's moving.

■ Years ago, when a person decided to live on a piece of land, one of the first things he did was to put down stakes. He drove sticks or posts into the ground to mark the boundaries of the property so that other people would know that this was his land. If he ever decided to move, he pulled up the stakes.

19. "Getting her to wear a dress is like **pulling teeth**."
It's very difficult to get her to do it when she doesn't want to.

■ Nobody ever went into a dentist's office and said, "Pull out my teeth, please." It's usually a painful experience. It's definitely something you don't want to do. Now pretend that you have to get somebody to do something, and she's resisting fiercely. You're just like the dentist, and she's just like the patient. It's just like "pulling teeth," isn't it? Ouch!

20. "He's really **playing with fire** now."
He's taking dangerous risks.

◼ You can play with a ball. You can play with blocks. You can play with all kinds of toys. But you'd better not play with fire! You'd be courting disaster. If anyone puts himself or herself into danger by taking unnecessary risks, then he or she is "playing with fire" and could get burned.

21. "She's the big shot, and he just **plays second fiddle** to her."
He's less important.

◼ Did you know that in an orchestra, the most important musician is the first violinist? He or she is called the concertmaster. You may have seen the conductor shaking hands with the first violinist at the end of a concert. Well, it's easy to figure out that if playing first fiddle is the most important job, "playing second fiddle" is a secondary, inferior job.

22. "She's just **playing cat and mouse** with him."
She's teasing him by pretending to let him go free, then catching him again.

■ Cats and mice are natural enemies. Cats usually catch mice. But if a cat is in a playful mood, he or she might fool a poor mouse by catching him, releasing him, then catching him again.

23. "When there's a big test, Cooky always **plays hooky**."
She stays home from school without an excuse.

■ Years ago, the slang word *hook* meant "escape." Today, if someone doesn't go to work or school and has no good excuse for his absence, we say he is "playing hooky" (which can also be spelled "hookie" and "hookey"). In a way, he has "escaped" from the place he didn't want to go to.

24. "She's very popular and always **plays the field**."
She has a lot of boyfriends.

■ Imagine a whole field full of race horses. If a gambler bets on just one horse, he might lose his money. But if he bets on many horses, if he "plays the field" of horses, a few horses are certain to win. Some people think that if you limit yourself to just one boyfriend or girlfriend, you can't be sure he or she is a "winner." So by "playing the field," you can meet more people and maybe find Mr. or Ms. Right.

25. "Don't believe him. He's just **playing possum**."
    He's pretending something to escape notice or to fool you.

    ■ Opossums are cunning animals. A possum can protect itself
    from another animal by lying so still for hours that the other animal
    thinks the possum is dead. Today, if someone pretends to be
    sleeping to get out of a job, or pretends not to know something in
    order to escape punishment, or stays very quiet so no one will
    know he's there, then he is copying the actions (or really the
    inactions) of a possum. He's "playing possum."

26. "In this book, we're **playing with words**."
    We're using words playfully and with double meanings.

    ■ When you make verbal jokes or puns with words, or stretch
    words to suggest different meanings or to achieve special effects
    (like a laugh or a gasp), you're "playing with words." Have fun!

·3·

Throw, Hit, Catch

27. "In the middle of the tough fight, he **threw in the towel**."
He gave up.

■ Like "pulling punches," this idiom comes from boxing. If a fighter was being badly beaten, his manager would throw into the ring the sponge or towel used to wipe the fighter between rounds. That meant that the fighter was giving up. Today, we use this idiom (with either "towel" or "sponge") to mean the same thing: to surrender in any kind of contest, debate, or election.

28. "Today she's **throwing her hat into the ring**."
She's announcing that she's a candidate for political office.

■ In America in the early 1800s, a man challenged another man by throwing his hat into a ring. The other man accepted the challenge by throwing his hat into the ring, too. Today, the idiom is used only for political contests. When you run for any public office, you have to "throw your hat into the ring."

29. "They **threw a party** last night, a wild party!"
They had a party.

■ You can have a party, hold a party, give a party, or make a party. Then why do we sometimes say that someone "threw a party"? It seems to suggest something a little more boisterous, a little noisier, and a little wilder, doesn't it? If you were trying to get a good night's sleep, you'd probably wish that the people upstairs were just having a party, not throwing one!

30. "She **threw a monkey wrench** into the project."
She did something to spoil the whole plan.

■ If you need to fix a piece of complicated machinery, one of the tools you might use is a monkey wrench. But if you threw that monkey wrench into the machine, fouling up all the gears and wheels, pulleys and valves, you might wreck it. Likewise, we say that if you interfere with a project that is going smoothly, you're "throwing a monkey wrench" into it.

31. "I like the idea, but he **threw cold water** on it."
He discouraged me.

■ Heat or fire has always suggested great enthusiasm or eagerness. If someone throws "cold water" on your burning emotions, then he's dampening your enthusiasm by dousing the "fire." He's a wet blanket!

32. "That kid **throws a temper tantrum** whenever he doesn't get his way."
He becomes angry and wild.

■ A temper tantrum is an angry outburst. A person has to be highly agitated or strongly excited to have one. Often, the person throws things around in a frenzy. Sometimes he throws himself around. Watch out!

33. "She's a lady who likes to **throw her weight around**."
She uses her influence in a showy manner.

■ To some people, weight suggests strength and position. We often think of a big person as a powerful person. In stories, a giant is usually more powerful than an ordinary person. So if someone is bossing around other people in a noisy or obvious way, we say he's "throwing his weight around." (By the way, you can be skinny and still "throw your weight around" if you act bossy.)

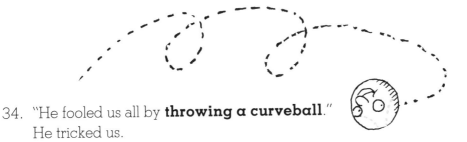

34. "He fooled us all by **throwing a curveball**."
He tricked us.

■ In baseball, when a pitcher throws a curveball, it looks like it's going straight, but then it curves unexpectedly. That can fool the batter. So if someone "throws you a curveball," he or she does something you don't expect in order to catch you off guard.

35. "That daredevil. He always **throws caution to the winds**."
He makes bold moves and takes big risks.

■ If you throw anything away ("to the winds"), you obviously don't care much about it. If you fling caution to the winds, you don't care much about safety or avoiding danger.

36. "He got so furious, he started to **hurl insults** at everyone."
He was shouting offensive remarks at people.

■ When you hurl something, you throw it forcefully, often violently. So when someone "hurls insults," he's obviously extremely angry to be throwing such hurtful and abusive insults all about.

37. "She's making extra money **slinging hash** at night."
She works as a waitress.

■ Hash once referred specifically to chopped meat and potatoes cooked together. Today, this word can mean any kind of cheap food, definitely not gourmet (fancy) delicacies. We say that a waiter or waitress who works in a small, plain restaurant, serving quick, low-cost meals, is "slinging hash"—throwing inexpensive food on the table.

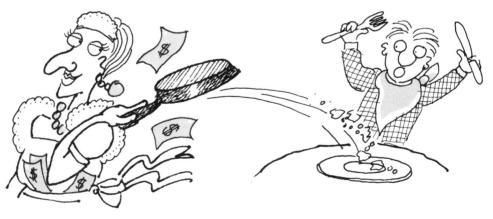

38. "That candidate certainly knows how to **sling mud**."
He knows how to say terrible things about his opponent.

■ "Mud" in this idiom doesn't mean wet dirt. It means filthy gossip, scandalous rumors, and vicious lies that are meant to damage the reputation of someone. Sometimes a desperate person tries to ruin another person's good name by "slinging mud" at him or her.

39. "C'mon, son. It's time to **hit the road**."
It's time to be on our way.

■ When you walk or run, you "hit the road" with the bottoms of your shoes or sneakers. When you drive or ride your bicycle, you "hit the road" with your tires. So, when you leave, get going, get on with your travels, or just move on, you're "hitting the road."

40. "It's past my bedtime. I'm going to **hit the hay** now."
I'm going to bed.

■ Early in American history, many cheap mattresses were filled with hay or straw. People who didn't have beds sometimes slept on grass in fields or on hay in barns. If you are really tired, you might just flop into bed. Your head hits the pillow, and your body hits the mattress. Hey, you've "hit the hay"!

41. "He's rich now. He **hit the jackpot**!"
He won a lot of money.

■ "Jack" is an old word for a playing card. Money bet on card games was sometimes kept in a pot on the table. So "jackpot" came to mean a top prize or high reward in a card game or any kind of contest. Today, if you "hit the jackpot," it won't hit you back. You'll probably be sensationally lucky, spectacularly successful, or fabulously wealthy. Lucky you!

42. "Your answer **hits the nail on the head**."
You're exactly right.

■ If you take careful aim with your hammer and hit the nail smack on its head so that it goes into the wood perfectly straight, you've done exactly the right thing. When you act in the most effective way, when you express the most accurate words, when you do something just the way it should be done, you've "hit the nail on the head." Congratulations!

43. "I'm **hitting the books** for the big test tomorrow."
I'm studying my school assignments.

■ Some people say they're doing their homework. Other people say they're "hitting the books." All of them are really doing the same thing, only the second phrase describes the studying more colorfully.

44. "That cold drink really **hits the spot**."
That satisfies me fully.

■ The "spot" in this idiom originally meant the bull's-eye at the center of a target. If you hit the bull's-eye with an arrow or a dart, you'd definitely be satisfied with yourself, wouldn't you? Suppose you're feeling sad, tired, hungry, or thirsty, and something (especially food or drink) picks you up. That something would "hit the spot." Bull's-eye!

45. "Let's **bat this idea around** before we tell the boss."
Let's discuss it in depth.

■ In a ball game, the pitcher throws the ball to the hitter, who bats it to the other players, who catch it and throw it around to one another. If people are discussing a plan, one person expresses an idea to another, who tells it to a third, who gives his opinions to a fourth, who criticizes it to a fifth, who praises it to a sixth person. That idea is being batted around just like a ball in a game.

46. "When I told him the astounding news, he didn't even **bat an eye lash**."
He didn't show the slightest degree of surprise.

■ Remember from idiom #4 that when people express surprise they often raise their eyebrows? Well, they can often flutter their eyelashes, too, especially when they're really shocked or amazed. But when people don't bat their eyelashes, that means they're showing no signs of shock, surprise, fear, or interest. What calm people!

47. "You're **batting a thousand** now!"
You're doing a perfect job.

■ Baseball players have batting averages based on the number of times they hit the ball when they're up at bat. Of course, nobody has ever batted a thousand, the perfect score. But if someone did, he'd be a perfect player.

48. "**Beat the bushes**. Find that man!"
Search everyplace.

■ Sometimes birds and small animals hide in the bushes to escape hunters. When hunters beat the bushes with sticks, they're trying to discover any game hiding in them. If you're searching diligently for someone or something in every possible place you can, then you're "beating the bushes," too.

49. "I can't stop now. I have to **beat the clock**."
I have to get everything done by a certain time.

■ When you're in a race, you have to beat your opponents at the finish line. When you're in a race with time, you have to "beat the clock" by the deadline. You have to accomplish all your tasks before your time runs out.

50. "That baby can howl to **beat the band**!"
His crying drowns out every other sound.

■ In the early 1900s, band concerts were extremely popular in American towns. No other kind of public entertainment could "beat the band." People would race to get to a parade before the band passed. Since the band usually led the other marchers and floats, if you "beat the band," you got there in time to see the whole parade.

51. "Every morning I have to **punch the clock** by 8:00 A.M."
I have to be at work by that time.

■ Some businesses have time clocks by their front doors. Employees have cards with their names on them. They insert the cards into a slot in the clock. The clock stamps the time on the card so that the boss will know when each worker came and went. Some workers may be angry at this system and want to give the clock a good punch, but "punching the clock" doesn't mean that. It means checking in and out with the time card.

52. "Her name **strikes a familiar chord**."
I remember it.

■ A chord is a group of notes played (or struck) together. If you've heard a chord before and recognize it when it's played, then it's a familiar chord. Today, we say that anything you hear—a name, a phrase, a thought—that you remember hearing before "strikes a familiar chord."

53. "That's too long. That's too short. That one **strikes a happy medium**."
That's the best possible compromise.

■ The medium is the middle. Imagine two possible solutions to a problem. However, neither solution will work because they're both too much. Then you find something halfway between the extremes that "hits the nail on the head." You've "struck a happy medium."

54. "He **struck it rich** in Texas!"
He suddenly became wealthy.

■ Imagine someone taking an ax, striking a chunk of rock, and finding gold. He's struck it rich! If you discover gold or oil or buried treasure, you'll be rich, too. "Striking it rich" is like "hitting the jackpot."

55. "The teacher is in a good mood. **Strike while the iron is hot**. Ask her to cancel the test."
Act when there's the best opportunity for success.

■ A metalworker knows that the best time to work on any metal is when it's very hot. For example, a blacksmith has to heat a bar of iron to a high temperature before he can strike it with his hammer and bend it into a horseshoe. So if there's a good opportunity to accomplish something, you had better "strike while the iron is hot." It's all in the timing.

56. "I'm so tired, I think I'll **catch forty winks**."
I'll take a little nap.

■ Forty has always been an important number. Ali Baba had forty thieves. In the Bible, it rained for forty days and forty nights. And if you're going to sleep long enough for your eyes to flutter only forty times, it's not going to be a long doze at all.

57. "Say it again, please. She didn't **catch on**."
She didn't understand what you said.

■ Imagine that when someone says something, he's throwing words out of his mouth. Imagine that when you understand what he says, you're catching his words with your ears. You're catching his meaning. You're "catching on."

VOTE FOR JOHNNY SLUG

58. "A pretty face always **catches my eye**."
It attracts my attention.

■ Something or someone doesn't really catch your actual eye, of course. People don't throw their eyes around. But when you catch sight of something that captures your attention, it's caught your vision (eye). Catch on?

○4○

Run, Jump, Kick

59. "They buy everything they like and **run up a big bill**."
They purchase a lot without thinking about the total cost.

■ When you recklessly run up too many bills, you're likely to run into debt. If you run into difficulty paying up, you'll probably want to run somewhere and hide. But the people you owe money to may run after you. Then you'll get run down. So, don't run up too many bills.

60. "He's **running a high temperature** and can't perform tonight."
His body temperature is higher than normal.

■ Most people have a normal body temperature of 98.6° F. If your temperature stays above that number for a long time, you're running a fever and someone should run for a doctor.

61. "Talent like that **runs in the family**."
Several people in that family have that talent.

■ When a certain characteristic is learned (like playing the violin) or inherited (like red hair) from other members of the same family, we say that the trait "runs in that family." Sometimes we even say it "runs in the blood."

62. "Every time I try to convince him, I **run into a stone wall**."
He absolutely refuses to change his mind.

■ Imagine actually running into a stone or brick wall. You wouldn't get very far, and it would certainly be a frustrating experience. The "stone wall" in this idiom refers to something (such as an idea or a belief) that is hard to overcome or to get someone to change.

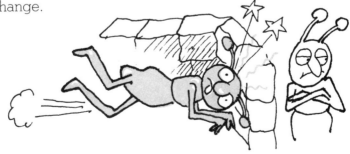

63. "She's so intelligent, she **runs rings around him**."
She is more skillful and can easily do the job much better.

■ If someone is standing still, he or she can't move forward, make progress, or get anywhere. Anyone who can run rings or circles around that person is obviously someone who can really move faster and accomplish more.

64. "Call the police. He's **running wild** again."
He's going berserk.

■ If someone in a state of frenzy dashes about without any self-control, rushing and rioting, we say he's "running amuck" or "running wild." You'd better run for help!

65. "She's **running a big risk** doing that."
She's putting herself in danger.

■ When you do something chancy or hazardous, and you don't protect yourself from harm, you're "running a risk." The risk could be physical (like walking a tightrope without a net below) or financial (like putting money into a questionable investment) or personal (like telling the boss you don't like his new plans).

66. "When he sees what's in there, he'll **jump out of his skin**."
He'll be terrified.

■ Nobody could actually jump right out of his skin, of course. But if you're badly frightened or very surprised, you might throw your hands up and scream loudly and appear to be trying to get away fast, faster than your skin can go.

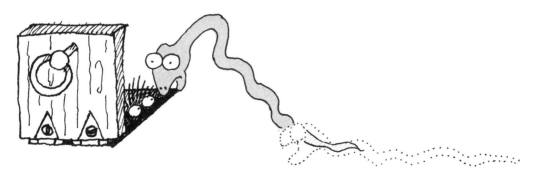

67. "He didn't wait for the signal. He **jumped the gun**."
He started before anyone else.

■ Often, a shot from a starter pistol begins a footrace or a swim meet. But if a person is so nervous or keyed up that he starts before the pistol shot, he's going before he should. He's "jumped the gun!" "Jumping the gun" can refer to anything started hastily before the scheduled time or before all preparations for it are made. You can also "jump the gun" if you want to be the first person to do something and beat the competition.

68. "Examine all the facts first, before you **jump to conclusions**."
You decide something without knowing all the facts.

■ Before you arrive at a decision, you should find out all the facts and think through the situation carefully. If you don't take these steps first, you're "jumping to conclusions" too quickly and possibly making a mistake.

69. "Think what you're doing! You're **jumping off the deep end**." You're making a drastic move without thinking it through.

■ Before you dive into a river or lake, you should make sure the water isn't too deep for you. Otherwise, you could be in serious trouble. In other areas of life, it is also important not to act rashly and without careful consideration. If the action you take is too risky, you might get into serious difficulty. It's like diving into water so far above your head that it's not safe.

70. "I can't stand his smoking. I wish he'd **kick the habit**." I wish he'd quit.

■ If you have a bad habit, something you'd like to stop doing, you should take that habit and give it such a good, hard kick that it flies far away from you and never comes back. That's just what this idiom means.

71. "That baby **kicks up a fuss** when her mother leaves her."
That baby complains angrily.

■ When babies make trouble, cause disturbances, or become too active, they often kick their legs wildly. Well, that idea of "kicking up a fuss" carries over into adulthood when grown-ups noisily demand action or quarrel loudly about something.

72. "Every New Year's Eve they really **kick up their heels**."
They really have a jolly time.

■ Horses that are high-spirited kick up their heels. You may have seen them in a circus. People who are celebrating merrily or dancing joyously often kick up their heels. Anyone who acts like a spirited child is "kicking up his heels." By the way, you don't actually have to dance to "kick up your heels." You can just be enjoying yourself in a high-spirited way.

73. "I asked him about that, but he just **sidestepped the issue**." He avoided the issue.

■ If you don't step right up to a problem and try to solve it, or if you don't answer a question directly, then you're stepping to one side and letting the matter pass you by. It's often better to get right to the heart of things and not sidestep them.

74. "I'd better buy it fast before he **hikes up the price**."
He raises the price.

■ A youngster can hike up his or her trousers (if they're dragging in the mud), a bus company can hike up its fares, and a landlord can hike up the rent. And if a store hikes up its prices too much, you can always hike to another store.

75. "I hope this picture will **jog his memory**."
I hope it will cause him to remember something.

■ To jog means to shake, push, even jolt. If something nudges or jostles your memory, it reminds you of something else.

·5·

Other Body Actions

With your fingers

76. "I love to dance when she **tickles the ivories**."
My feet can't stop moving when she plays the piano.

■ The "ivories" in this phrase are the keys on a piano. Some people pound the keys. Others merely tap them. But a good pianist "tickles the ivories" and makes the piano laugh with music.

77. "He's her favorite boyfriend because he **tickles her fancy**."
He pleases her a lot.

■ Your fancy can be your imagination or your special fondness for something. So when someone "tickles your fancy," he or she amuses you greatly. It is also said that when something pleases or entertains you, you're "tickled to death" or "tickled pink."

78. "I wish he'd stop **bending her ear**."
I wish he'd stop talking so much.

■ If someone just talks and talks endlessly and boringly, your ear never really bends, of course. But you can imagine how it could with all those words going around and into it.

79. "A sweet smile can make him **bend the rules**."
It can make him change the regulations.

■ A rule is supposed to be as rigid as a bar of iron, and people are supposed to obey rules strictly. But if someone "bends" a rule by changing it slightly, the rule is no longer rigid. A lot of people try to bend the rules, and some even break them!

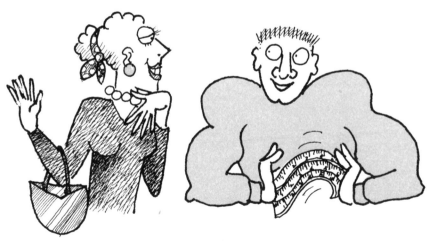

80. "This newspaper article only **scratches the surface** of the story."
It tells only a few facts, not the whole story.

■ A scratch is a very light cut in something. It doesn't go very deeply beneath the surface. So anything that only "scratches the surface" doesn't penetrate much. It's an answer that gives only part of the explanation. It's a tale that tells very little of the story. It's a clue that solves only a bit of the mystery.

81. "The professors can never agree. They're always **splitting hairs**."
They're quarreling about very unimportant matters.

■ A hair is an exceptionally thin strand. If you split a hair, the pieces would be even thinner. Today, we say that people who split hairs are arguing about extremely minor differences in things as if these trivial distinctions were really important. People have been using this idiom for three hundred years. That's a lot of split hairs!

82. "I'll **touch base** with you next week."
I'll contact you.

■ A baseball player has to touch first, second, and third base quickly in order to arrive safely at home plate and score a run. Similarly, if, every once in a while, you call up a friend, or send him a note, or drop in to see him, you're "touching base" with him. You're making brief contact.

With your arms

83. "If she keeps doing that, I'll **press charges** against her."
I'll accuse her of a crime.

■ One of the many meanings of "press" is to force someone to act, to urge on. When you "press charges," you formally charge someone with criminal activity. You press the police to arrest him. You press the court to indict him. You press the jury to convict him. You press the judge to sentence him. You put on a lot of pressure!

84. "He's really **pressing his luck** if he thinks he can do that."
He's depending too much on just luck to get him through this difficult situation.

■ If you think your luck is never going to run out, you'd better beware. If you press—that is, force—your luck too far, it might not be able to stand the pressure. That would be unlucky!

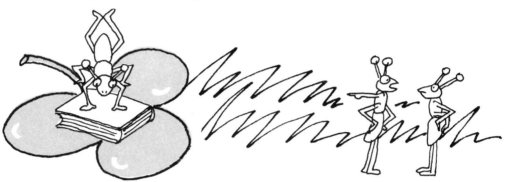

85. "The mayor has to **press the flesh** at election time."
He shakes a lot of hands.

■ The "flesh" in this idiom refers to the skin on the inside of people's hands. This expression is usually said or written about politicians running for office. They have to greet a lot of people to get votes. They try to shake hands with everyone they meet. That's a lot of flesh getting pressed.

86. "That's just Uncle Joe, **sawing logs**."
He's snoring.

■ Think what it sounds like when someone saws logs. Think what it sounds like when a sleeping person breathes loudly through his or her nose. Some imaginative writer or speaker once thought that these two sounds were similar. That's why today we say that a sleeping person with a noisy nose is "sawing logs."

87. "Susie is our best reporter. She always **scoops the news**."
She gets the news stories first.

■ When you scoop an object up, you lift it out with something like a small shovel. You can scoop out ice cream or mashed potatoes or sand. If you're a reporter, you can also "scoop the news" if you're the first one to dig out a story. You scoop the competition when you publish or broadcast the story before any other newspaper or news program does.

88. "Freddie Fib always **stretches the truth**."
He exaggerates.

■ When you tell the truth, you tell exactly what happened. The truth is not stretchable like a rubber band. But if someone "stretches the truth," he's adding untrue parts to the story. Someone can also "stretch a point" by making an exception or exaggerating.

89. "David feels bad today, so Jennifer is **stroking his ego**."
She's saying or doing things that make him feel good about himself.

■ When you stroke your pet, you move your hand gently over the animal in a soothing way. "Ego" comes from the Latin word for "I." Your ego is your self-esteem. It's what you think of yourself. When someone strokes your ego, he praises and flatters you and makes you feel good about yourself.

90. "Grandma always **holds court** with her relatives."
She acts like a queen with her subjects.

■ The word "court" in this idiom could refer to either a royal court or a courtroom. When someone acts like a very important person, and other people let him, then he's "holding court." He's behaving like a king or a judge—regal or legal—giving advice and telling people what to do.

91. "**Hold your horses**, Harold! Don't get so excited."
Don't rush ahead.

■ Suppose you are driving a team of horses. They start to run too fast. You pull on the reins and hold your horses back. We use this same phrase to advise someone to be patient, to hold back from just rushing ahead and doing something without thinking. In the same way, we can tell someone to "hold your tongue" (don't say anything) or "hold your temper" (stay calm).

With your whole body

92. "Wanda's **wrestling with her conscience** again."
She's trying to decide what to do.

■   In wrestling, two opponents struggle hand to hand. One tries to force the other to the ground. If you're "wrestling with your conscience," you're trying to decide how to act. Maybe your conscience is telling you to do one thing, but you want to do another. It's like a wrestling match.

93. "C'mon, boys! Let's **tackle this job**."
Let's do it!

■   A football player tackles another player by grabbing him and throwing him to the ground. Similarly, when you "tackle a tough job," you roll up your sleeves and go to it. Like the football player, you're trying to get hold of the tough chore and overcome it.

94. "Beulah really **bowls people over**!"
She stupefies and astounds them.

◼ When you go bowling, you try to knock over as many pins as you can with a big ball. In life, you can "bowl people over" by surprising them with what you say, by dumfounding them by what you do, or by astonishing them by what you wear. It's as though you were knocking down the surprised people with a huge bowling ball.

95. "Clara always **climbs the walls** when she has to work late."
She feels terribly restless and wants to get out.

◼ If you feel trapped in a place and are getting so nervous and frustrated that you just have to get out, you might try to climb the walls to escape. People have really done that. In much the same way, if someone has to do a long, boring job, or if he's stuck in some awful place, he might start feeling extremely tense. He's "climbing the walls" because he wants relief from what is making him so anxious.

96. "The ambassador **drives a hard bargain**."
He's a tough negotiator.

■ One meaning of "drive" is to force someone into a condition: "That noise is driving me crazy!" It can also mean to strike something: "The carpenter drives the nail." It can mean to overwork: "She's been driving herself too hard." This idiom can also mean to arrive at an agreement (usually in business or politics) after a lot of hard negotiating. If your terms are tough and you stick to them, you're "driving a hard bargain."

97. "Instead of tackling the problem, he prefers to **duck the issue**."
He avoids it entirely.

■ If someone yells, "Duck!" you lower your head quickly because you don't want to be hit by something hurtling through the air. Now suppose there's a difficult subject you should deal with. But you don't want to. You want to escape from it. So you "duck the issue" by not answering questions about it, by refusing to try to solve it, or by just pretending it doesn't exist. "Ducking an issue" is like sidestepping it.

98. "I asked who will do this, but they all tried to **dodge responsibility**."
They all said it's not their job.

■ When you play dodgeball, you duck and dart every which way to keep from being hit by the ball. If a person "dodges responsibility," he uses trickery and cunning to pretend he is not the one who is really supposed to do something. He says he's not the cause of it. He is not accountable for it. A person can also "dodge duties" or "dodge a question."

°6°

A Lockerful of Exercise Idioms

exercise caution

exercise the duties

exercise your rights
exercise patience

exercise your options

exercise discretion

When you exercise, you can do push-ups, jog, lift weights, swim, or perform other physical activities to keep fit. But "exercise" can also have other meanings. So not only can you exercise your body, you can also **exercise the duties** of president. You can **exercise your rights** as a citizen. You can **exercise your authority** as boss. You can **exercise patience** in a trying situation. You can **exercise caution** when there's danger around. You can **exercise your options** when you choose among different courses of action. And you can **exercise discretion** when you use good judgment, especially when you keep secrets. With all that exercising, you'll be in great shape!

Alphabetical List of the
Idioms in This Book

61

Other Books About Idioms

If you want to learn more about idioms, you might like to read some of the following books that the author used in his research.

Boatner, Maxine Tull, and Gates, John Edward, **A Dictionary of American Idioms**, Woodbury, New York: Barron's Educational Series, Inc., 1975.

Chapman, Robert L., editor, **American Slang**, New York: Harper & Row, 1987.

Collis, Harry, **American English Idioms**, Lincolnwood, Illinois: Passport Books, 1986.

Funk, Charles Earle, **A Hog on Ice & Other Curious Expressions**, New York: Harper & Row, Colophon Edition, 1985.

Rogers, James, **The Dictionary of Cliches**, New York: Ballantine Books, 1987.

Rosenthal, Peggy, and Dardess, George, **Every Cliche in the Book**, New York: William Morrow and Company, Inc., 1987.

Spears, Richard A., **NTC's American Idioms Dictionary**, Lincolnwood, Illinois: National Textbook Company, 1988.

Terban, Marvin, **In a Pickle and Other Funny Idioms**, New York: Clarion Books, 1983.

Terban, Marvin, **Mad As a Wet Hen! and Other Funny Idioms**, New York: Clarion Books, 1987.

Wentworth, Harold, and Flexner, Stuart Berg, **The Pocket Dictionary of American Slang**, New York: Pocket Books, 1968.

Whitford, Harold C., and Dixson, Robert J., **Handbook of American Idioms and Idiomatic Usage**, New York: Regents Publishing Company, Inc., 1973.

About the Author

Marvin Terban has been teaching English for twenty-five years at Columbia Grammar and Preparatory School in New York City where many of his word play books began as grammar games in his classroom. He lives in an apartment overlooking a Central Park playground with his wife, Karen, also a teacher, and their two children, David, 18, and Jennifer, 14.

About the Artist

Born in Cincinnati, Tom Huffman grew up in Lexington, Kentucky, and received a degree in fine arts from the University of Kentucky. He now lives in New York City and has illustrated other books for Clarion including *The Dove Dove* by Marvin Terban and *Be a Perfect Person in Just Three Days!* by Stephen Manes.